Going to School

These children are arriving at school.

They enjoy meeting their friends. Together they learn to read and write, and do number work. They learn many other skills too.

Headteacher

The headteacher runs the school.

Mrs Brady does not teach a class, but she likes to look at the children's work. These children have brought their best work to her room. She will give them a gold star.

Mrs Brady is giving out awards and certificates at assembly.

There is always a special **assembly** on Friday. It is led by one class. These children have been chosen by their teacher because they worked very hard or behaved very well this week.

Secretaries

Mrs Smith, a school secretary works in the office.

She is typing a **newsletter** for parents. She also uses her computer to print out orders for equipment. Mrs Smith does the **accounts** at the end of the year.

When children have lost something or need help, they come to Mrs Davis at the office.

They can also buy equipment. Rachel is wearing a school purse-belt to keep her money safe. Luke is buying a plastic swimming bag for his kit. He will mark it with his name.

Class Teachers

Mrs Inman is a reception class teacher and is watching over a group using the sand tray.

The children are playing happily together, sharing the equipment and finding out what they can do with it. Some of the class are learning by water play. Others are learning to build with **construction** kits.

Mrs Clark is helping a group of Year 2 children with reading.

They are following the story from a book with large print and pictures, which they can all see. Shareen is pointing out the words as she reads aloud.

Miss Scott is helping the children to make wooden boxes.

They are using special equipment. The goggles **protect** their eyes. They have sawing blocks to help them to cut the wood and to protect the table.

Mr Hurst and some of his class are taking part in an activity called circle time.

Everyone in the group has to watch and listen very carefully. Rebecca is **miming** actions. The others will take it in turn to copy her and to add to the mime.

Special Needs Teachers

Miss Harris helps some of the children with reading, writing or number work.

These children are reading in pairs. An older child is helping a younger child learn to read. They are happy to help the younger children as they used to find reading difficult, too.

Miss Stone is working with children who do not speak English at home.

The children are matching picture cards. They enjoy naming the animals. Natasha speaks English well. She likes to help the others.

The School Crossing Patrol

The school crossing patrol helps children to cross the road safely.

There are many parked cars, so it is hard to see the traffic. Mrs Fox wears a special **uniform**. She holds up a sign telling the cars to stop.

First Aider

Mrs Lunn is looking after children who have hurt themselves in the playground.

She is **trained** in First Aid but Mrs Lunn does not give any medicines. If a child has a bad accident, she will tell the parents. They will take the child to the doctor or to hospital.

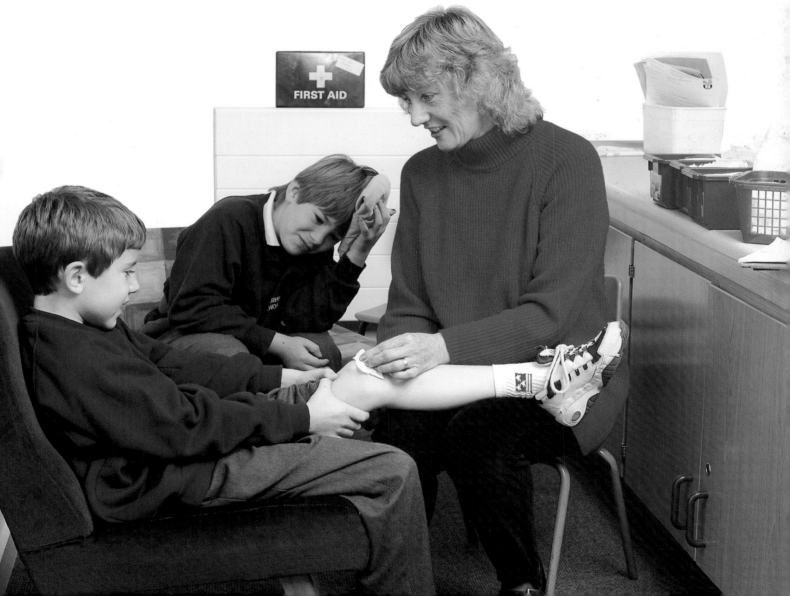

Caretaker

The school caretaker is fixing new clothes pegs.

Mr Allen keeps the school building safe and makes sure that everything works properly. After school, he checks that all the rooms are locked and that the lights are turned off.

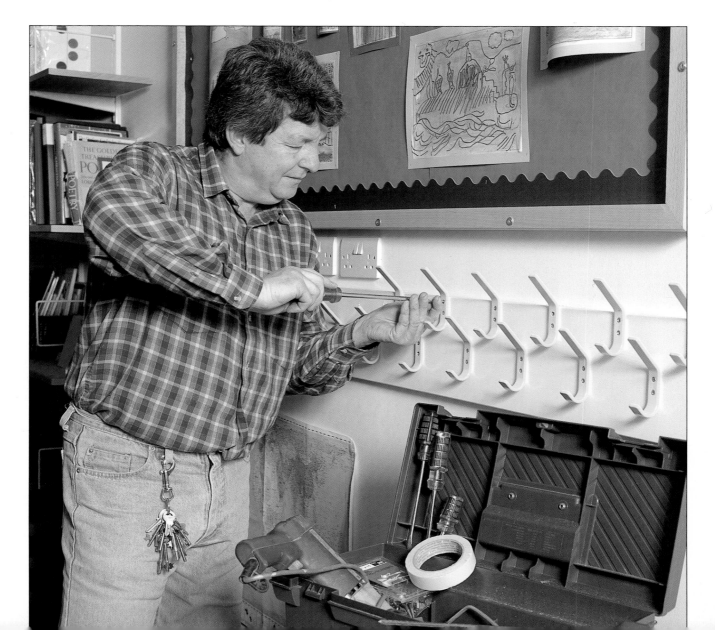

Cleaners

Mrs Husen is one of the cleaners who tidies up after school and vacuums each classroom.

The children help to keep the classroom tidy. At the end of the day, they stack the chairs and put away the equipment.

Kitchen Staff

Mrs Price and her team of helpers make more than two hundred hot meals every day.

Children can choose from a wide **menu**. The kitchen staff help them to decide on a balanced meal. Children need a good dinner at midday to give them energy, and to do well at school.

Dinner Staff

Mrs Robins helps to make sure dinner time runs smoothly and calmly.

She watches children put the waste food into the bin. They stack their dirty plates and put the **cutlery** into special bowls. Mrs Robins will wipe the trays clean.

Support Teachers

Mrs Rose is one of the support teachers.

She enjoys helping pupils work with the computers.

The support teachers helped by the caretaker, keep playtime happy. Mrs Rose is helping some children with a problem.

Playground Duty Staff

There are always teachers on duty at break time.

There are **rules** to make sure children go back to class quietly. Mrs Jones blows her whistle once for them to stop playing and stand still. At the second whistle, they line up in their classes.

Parent Helpers

The school has many parent helpers who come and help at school.

James is showing Mrs McNab which book he is borrowing to read at home. Mrs McNab also helps to **catalogue** the books on a computer. Other parent helpers assist with spelling.

Governors

These two parent governors have joined a class on a visit to the park.

The parent governors also visit the school. Mrs Asare and Mr Henley are part of a team of sixteen governors. They help the headteacher to run the school.

Club Leaders

Mrs Green enjoys taking a singing group during the dinner hour.

These children enjoy learning to sing well together in the **choir**. They perform to parents and friends at concerts. At Christmas they sing carols at a local old people's home.

Mr Brown is keen on sport and runs a weekly gym club after school.

The pupils like using the apparatus and improving their skills. They learn to work together as a team when they put on displays at school **events**.

An art club is run after school by Mrs Hide.

She is helping a group of children with their **collage**. The children love using different materials and having more time to make things. Their artwork will be on **exhibition** in a town gallery.

Mr Weems is an actor and runs a drama club in the hall after school.

The children act out ideas, mime, and learn to work together. At the end of the year they will perform a play in **costume** for their parents and the rest of the school.

Topic Web

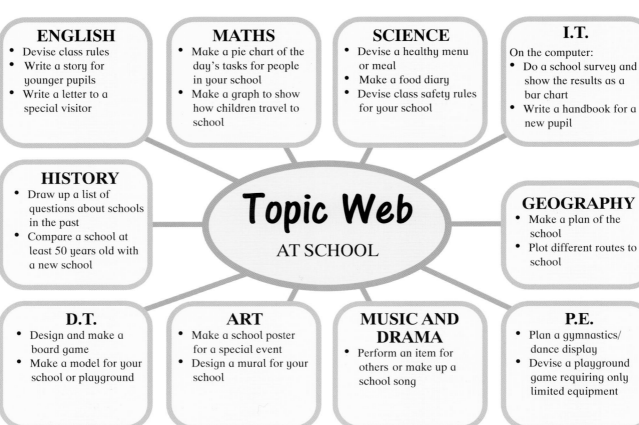

ENGLISH
- Devise class rules
- Write a story for younger pupils
- Write a letter to a special visitor

MATHS
- Make a pie chart of the day's tasks for people in your school
- Make a graph to show how children travel to school

SCIENCE
- Devise a healthy menu or meal
- Make a food diary
- Devise class safety rules for your school

I.T.
On the computer:
- Do a school survey and show the results as a bar chart
- Write a handbook for a new pupil

HISTORY
- Draw up a list of questions about schools in the past
- Compare a school at least 50 years old with a new school

Topic Web
AT SCHOOL

GEOGRAPHY
- Make a plan of the school
- Plot different routes to school

D.T.
- Design and make a board game
- Make a model for your school or playground

ART
- Make a school poster for a special event
- Design a mural for your school

MUSIC AND DRAMA
- Perform an item for others or make up a school song

P.E.
- Plan a gymnastics/ dance display
- Devise a playground game requiring only limited equipment

Notes for Teachers
The book aims to show children at Key Stage 1 and lower Key Stage 2 the roles of people who help them at school, through the jobs they perform. The book is mostly relevant to the PSE curriculum and also includes some elements of health education. The book emphasizes the importance of teamwork, encouraging children to co-operate in work and play. It will help them to develop an understanding of why school rules are made, and learn to practise ways of keeping safe and finding help from the appropriate adults.

In the schools shown in this book many of the adults have dual roles. The support teachers help in the dining room and at playtime, as does the caretaker. The first aider is a support teacher. The cleaners have children at the school. This strengthens teamwork and discipline, and makes for a supportive atmosphere.

Incorporating circle time (p. 11) into the curriculum also helps to build a supportive environment in which the emotional needs of children can be met. It is a way of raising any problems they have at school, or other issues. Everyone is involved in co-operative tasks, such as games, rounds or drama. Many circle time strategies are based on 'stories' that children develop, expand or discuss. Building self-esteem is a central aim. See *Turn Your School Round* (Books to Read, p. 31).

Paired reading (p. 12), both at home and at school, provides an opportunity for co-operation and support from parents and other pupils, giving confidence to those who have difficulties with reading and enabling them to gain pleasure from the written page. The older child reads to the younger one, and the younger child joins in whenever he or she is able to.

When working with wood (p. 10), it is helpful as a safety aid for a teacher to draw outlines of specialist tools and equipment on paper on the table or workbench where the children are working. This makes for an orderly, safe working environment, and makes it easy to check that no equipment has been misplaced.

Topics for discussion
Initially much discussion can be shared as to how this school differs from yours: the building, its situation, pupil numbers, staff, school rules and the reward system. Who do children go to for help if they are hurt, have a problem at playtime, or have lost or found something? Other topics might include: children's property: why does it need to be labelled? Safety: what safety signs are necessary in your school? Governors: how many school governors are there? How do they earn their living? Visitors: who comes into your school to help? For example, visitors from the fire service, police force, charities, nurses to make eye, ear and dental inspections. The P.T.A: how does it help the school? Uniforms: which people have a uniform and why? (Cook, Crossing Patrol). Does the school have a uniform and why?

Topic web activities

ENGLISH
• Speaking and Listening   • Writing

Imagine you are the headteacher of your school. Plan rules that your school should follow, for example, in the playground, in the dining hall, moving around the school. Write and illustrate a story to be read to a group of younger children.

Write a thank you letter to eg a school governor.

Provide opportunities for children to show visitors around the school.

MATHS
• Number: Collecting, representing and interpreting data

Make a pie chart to show how long people such as the headteacher, a teacher and a secretary spend doing each task during one day.

Make a graph to show how the children in your class come to school – by foot, bicycle, car, bus. How many come unaccompanied?

SCIENCE
• Humans as organisms   • Health and safety

Devise a healthy packed lunch that the children in the class would enjoy. Make sure that you include protein, carbohydrates, fruit, vegetables and a drink in your meal. Make a food diary for a week.

Find out what safety rules the school or class already has. In groups, assess safe and unsafe places around the school. Compare the lists made by the different groups.

I.T.
• Communicating and handling information

Choose three different school meals and ask all the children in the class which they would prefer to eat. Show this information on a bar chart. Find out which is the most popular meal eaten by the class in one day or one week.

Design and produce a small illustrated handbook about your school/class, to be given to new pupils at school.

HISTORY
• Historical enquiry

Prepare a list of questions to ask a grandparent or governor about his or her schooldays, e.g. What did children wear to school? How was the classroom arranged? How many children were there in a class? What lessons were taught? Invite a grandparent to school to answer questions.

Compare a school building from 50 years ago with one today. What has changed and what hasn't? For example, are the toilets indoors or outdoors? Are the ceilings and windows high or low?

GEOGRAPHY
• Geographical skills   • Mapping

On your school plan, label rooms and other areas, and the adults who use them. Plot the route from your classroom to various rooms.

Using a local street map, plot the routes taken by different children to school and work out who has the longest/shortest journey.

D.T
• Designing skills   • Making skills

Design and make a board game for younger pupils, based on the safety rules for your school

Design and make a model for an activity area and for a quiet area in the playground or school grounds.

ART
• Investigating and making

Make a poster for a special event at school such as a concert, art exhibition or dance display.

Design a mural incorporating special features about the history of your school and its surroundings.

MUSIC AND DRAMA
• Performing and composing

Compose, sing and play an item to be performed for others. Think carefully about the kind of song you would make up about your school. Which musical instruments will accompany your song?

P.E.
• Games, gymnastic activities, dance

Plan a gymnastics or dance display to be performed to an invited audience.

Using limited equipment, plan and devise a circuit of games/activities for a group of younger children.

Glossary

accounts A record of how much the school has spent and how much money has come in.

assembly When the whole school meets together.

catalogue To make a list of items.

choir People who sing together in a group.

collage Artwork made from pieces of paper, cloth, photos and anything else the artist wants to use.

construction Anything that is put together by building.

costume Special clothes worn by actors in a play.

cutlery Knives, forks and spoons used when eating at a table.

events Special occasions like a fête or concert.

exhibition A public display of works of art.

menu A list of dishes cooked that day.

miming To act without speaking.

newsletter A printed letter about what is going on at school.

protect To keep safe, or take care of something.

rules Ways of doing things that everyone follows.

trained When someone has practised and learned a skill.

uniform Special clothes worn to show what job a person does, or the school a child goes to.

Books to read

For children:
Our Schools by S. Ross, Starting History series
(Wayland, 1992)
School Day by M. Stoppleman, Turn of the Century
series (A & C Black, 1990)

For teachers:
The Cooperative Classroom and *Inside the Cooperative
Classroom* by Jane Gilmore and Patrick Dymond
(Links Educational Publications, 1996)
Turn Your School Round by Jenny Mosley (L.D.A., 1993)

Series editor: Sarah Doughty
Text editor: Cath Senker
Cover designer: Jan Sterling
Designer and typesetter: Malcolm Walker
Commissioned photography: APM (Andrew Perris)

First published in Great Britain in 1998
by Wayland Publishers Ltd
This paperback edition published in 2001
by Hodder Wayland, an imprint of
Hodder Children's Books

The author and publisher would like to thank
the staff and pupils at Davigdor Infants School
and Somerhill Junior School in Hove, Sussex.
All names of staff and pupils have been changed.

**British Library Cataloguing in Publication
Data**
Burt, Erica
   People who help us at school
   1. School employees – Juvenile literature
   I. Title II. At school
   372.1

ISBN 0 7502 3806 2

Printed and bound by EuroGrafica, Vicenza,
Italy

Index